Stories from the Old Testament

Book 5

Numbers and Deuteronomy

A Comic Book of Doggerel

for

Children of All Ages

FRED WURLITZER, M.D., F.A.C.S.

Numbers and Deuteronomy: A Comic Book of Doggerel

Publishing Details

Paperback Color Edition 1 / November 2020

ISBN: 978-1-716-43698-7

Imprint: Lulu.com

All Rights Reserved.

Copyright @ 2020 Fred Wurlitzer

No part of this book may be reproduced or transmitted in any form or by any means, electronic or mechanical, including such methods as photocopying, recording, or any information storage and retrieval system, without permission in writing from the author.

Images

All images in this book were downloaded from the Internet. Some were labeled as having User Rights as "For Reuse With or Without Modification," some were downloaded from the free image site, [Sweet Publishing.](#) The publishing rights for others were purchased from [Shutterstock.com.](#)

Books by Fred Wurlitzer

Poetry

The Gospel of Fred – 2019

The Second Gospel of Fred - 2019

Love to the Trinity – 2020

Non-Fiction

Rembert – 2020

(Includes the play, *Rembert*)

Children's Books

Spiritual Fairy Tales – 2020

The Seven Deadly Sins – 2020

The Seven Heavenly Virtues – 2020

Stories from the Old Testament

Comic Books with Doggerel

Book 1   *Genesis - Part 1* – 2020

Book 2   *Genesis - Part 2* – 2020

Book 3   *Exodus - Part 1* – 2020

Book 4   *Exodus - Part 2* – 2020

Book 5 - *Numbers and Deuteronomy* – 2020

Table of Contents

Numbers 1

    Miriam and Aaron Oppose Moses 3

    Twelve Spies Sent into Canaan 17

    The Serpent of Brass 41

Deuteronomy 63

    Moses Dies and Joshua Becomes Leader 65

Conclusion 87

Numbers and Deuteronomy: A Comic Book of Doggerel

Preface

   Judeo-Christianity is the largest religious group in the world. With over one-billion followers, the demand for children's books reflecting Judeo-Christianity is humongous. Yet, on *Amazon*, less than two dozen religious books for children with an orientation towards Judeo-Christianity are listed. None could be found with poetry, although there were possibly some historically.

   The poetry in this proposed book is in the style of Ogden Nash. It is not great poetry. It is relatively simple in a manner suitable for a child or adults appreciating child-like thinking. Hopefully, some of the poetry will be interesting to a young child or a child of any age.

   Sometimes when writing doggerel in the style of Ogden Nash, rhyming leads to surprising interpretations. For example, "The Lord will not forsake you. Let Him stick to you like glue."

   There are other examples that the reader will encounter, I hope, with tolerance and appreciation for the humor I intend to impart.

   When I use quotes, I am not quoting a Bible version. Many times in the Old Testament, exact quotes are not given. I am taking liberty interpreting what a biblical character may have said. The stories in the Old Testament are presented without quotes in most instances. This book is not meant to undermine in any way the Christian faith and gospel.

   A Biblical literalist might complain that I am altering Biblical language. I prefer to think that I am interpreting Biblical language in a slightly different, but entirely consistent manner with what the Bible intended. Our intent has been to remix, transform, and build upon the material given by the *freebibleimages* organization for the specific purpose of spreading Bible messages.

All the children's religious books on Amazon are heavily illustrated. This sixth book of our "small book" series called *Numbers and Deuteronomy* incorporates copyrighted illustrations from the Internet on a pay-for-usage basis. Some pictures were taken from the Internet site http://www.freebibleimages.org or were found and downloaded from searches where User Rights were marked as "Labeled for Reuse" or Labeled for Reuse with Modification." I feel indebted to the *freebibleimages* organization.

I feel indebted to the *freebibleimages* organization for its illustrations that we have used. These illustrations are being used for the purposes of spreading Bible stories to all people, but especially children.

Leviticus is not included with *Numbers and Deuteronomy*, because it deals with Old Testament laws that most people today would find archaic and largely irrelevant. Moreover, *Leviticus* covers no narratives about Israelite wanderings after they left Egypt.

The main thrusts of *Genesis*, *Exodus*, *Numbers* and *Deuteronomy* that entertain me are those chapters dealing with Israelite wanderings. Parts of *Numbers* that deal with a census, camp arrangements, and other legal matters are also not included for the same reason as not being relevant to most readers today.

When the author asked his wife if he should make the book bigger with more doggerel, her reply was simple, "Keep it small." We did that with our earlier little books for children. In this instance, we didn't keep the book small, but my wife still liked the book. Because of all the pictures and cartoons, we consider it a "big" little comic book. This series is our big little book of our comic book Bible series for children of all ages.

Numbers and *Deuteronomy* ("ND") relates the end adventures of a prophet named Moses, told originally by himself. It continues with adventures in the Promised Land when Joshua led the Israelites. It matters little whether one is religious or not reading ND if one is interested in reading great historical literature. It is a must-read.

Nonbelievers may view that because ND refers to God many times, it is not worthy of reading. "I won't be proselytized," they may say, so they turn their heads childishly away from great literature. They'll read works written about the same time, The Odyssey or The Iliad by Homer, near the end of the eighth century BCE, but not *Genesis*, *Exodus* or *Numbers and Deuteronomy*, which are ascribed to Moses around the sixth or fifth century BC or unknown authors during the Babylonian exile reflecting oral traditions.

I hope to take a reader away from biblical language that is sometimes stilted. By using doggerel and cartoons, this comic book will be readable for children of all ages.

I happen to believe sincerely in God. I trust that belief will not offend the reader. Like many other believers, as well as nonbelievers, I have difficulty personally reconciling Old Testament harshness with present day progressive thinking. Some harshness is in Exodus.

I hope that with illustrations and doggerel, children and adults thinking like children will be still entertained.

The first five books of the Bible, called "The Pentateuch" or "The Torah," will be covered eventually.

Fred Wurlitzer

Numbers and Deuteronomy are the fourth and fifth books of the Pentateuch or Torah. Other little Bible books will follow, and with illustrations and doggerel, I hope children of all ages will be entertained.

.

Numbers and Deuteronomy

A Comic Book of Doggerel
for
Children of All Ages

FRED WURLITZER, M.D., F.A.C.S.

Numbers and Deuteronomy: A Comic Book of Doggerel

NUMBERS

Numbers and Deuteronomy: A Comic Book of Doggerel

Miriam and Aaron Oppose Moses

Numbers 12:1-16

Numbers and Deuteronomy: A Comic Book of Doggerel

After Moses wed a Black, relations became strained.
Moses' sister Miriam and brother Aaron complained.

Color did not matter to Moses and laws he gathered.
It was respect and love for the Lord that mattered.

Moses explained:

"The Lord feels we and foreigners are the same.
Aliens who live with us have our rules by acclaim."[1]

Moses' bride from the Sudan loved the Lord.
She became a Hebrew through Moses' accord.

---
[1] Numbers 15:15–16

Numbers and Deuteronomy: A Comic Book of Doggerel

Miriam and Aaron challenge Moses:

"Has the Lord only spoken to Moses?" they asked.
"Hasn't he also spoken through us?" they blasted.

"Your bride is from a different nation.
We must membership with us, ration."

Fred Wurlitzer

Moses replied, "I am open to all foreign memberships,
Provided aliens accept like us the same legal scripts."

Numbers and Deuteronomy: A Comic Book of Doggerel

**Now Moses was a very humble man.
He had numerous, loyal Hebrew fans.**

The Lord invited all three to meet at a nearby tent.
He was more than upset with the bilious discontent.

The Lord attended in a cloud at the entrance
He was ready to render a sentence of penance.

"Step forward," the Lord said to Aaron and Miriam.
He confirmed the two had developed a mad delirium.

The Lord was angry with both of them.
He was prepared to compose a requiem.

To Miriam, God said, "You like being white skinned?
I'll make your skin really white to prove you sinned."

Fred Wurlitzer

When the cloud left, Miriam's skin was truly white. It was leprous, resulting from the Lord's just might.

Numbers and Deuteronomy: A Comic Book of Doggerel

**Moses pleaded with the almighty Lord.
"Make her clean; put away your sword."**

Fred Wurlitzer

The Lord said exile her for seven days.
She will be shamed until her eyes glaze.

When she returned, her skin was clean.
She was treated again like a holy queen.

She was, after all, Moses' beloved sister.
He didn't want her to have a skin blister.

Numbers and Deuteronomy: A Comic Book of Doggerel

Twelve Spies Sent into Canaan

Numbers 13:1-14:45

Numbers and Deuteronomy: A Comic Book of Doggerel

On the way to Canaan, Hebrews stopped a bit in Zin.
It was noteworthy that they had often been with sin.

It was at a place called Kadesh Barnea.
Ever far-sighted, Moses had no myopia.

Fred Wurlitzer

**God told Moses to pick a leader from every tribe.
Twelve men would be spies, Canaan to describe.**

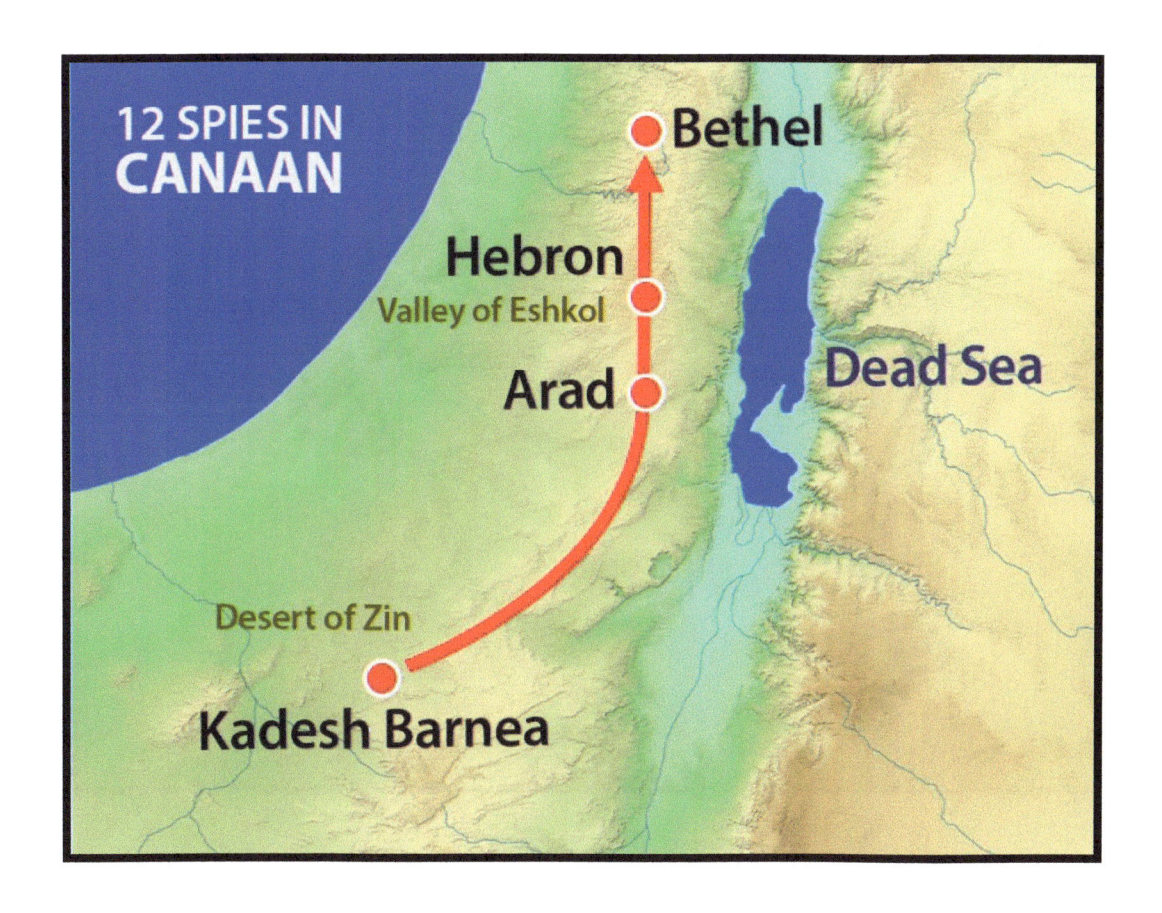

They would scout out the Canaan land ahead.
Was it truly a blessed land of honey and bread?

The twelve were Shammua, Shaphat, Caleb, Igal, Joshua, Palt and Gaddiel.

Several more were selected – Gaddi, Ammiel, Sethur, Nahbi and Geuel.

**Find out if the people are strong or weak.
We don't want to be going up a big creek.

How big are their towns and what is fortified?
We want to avoid experiencing any downside.

Is the soil fertile or poor?
Is there any good pasture?**

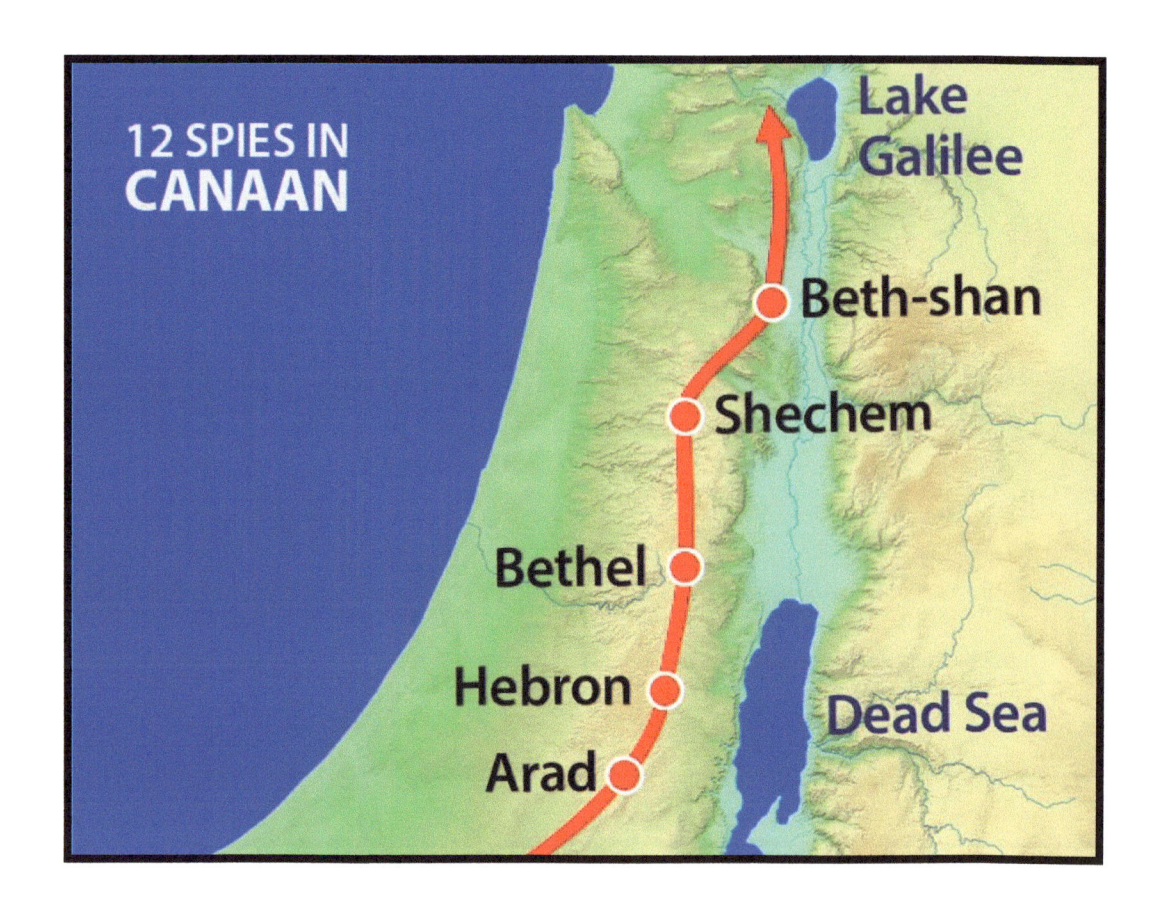

Bring back some fruit to taste.
Don't feel you must be in haste.

The twelve spies went pass the Negev desert.
As they traveled, they were ever on the alert.

From there they passed the Amalekites up into hills.
They certainly were not looking for foothill thrills.

They saw strong people, heirs of Anak.

They felt it foolish to ever them attack.

They went north past Hittites, Jebusites, Amorites,
Then the River Jordan and Lake Galilee to Canaanites.

The towns and cities were large and well-fortified. Settling in Canaan would not be a mirthful joyride.

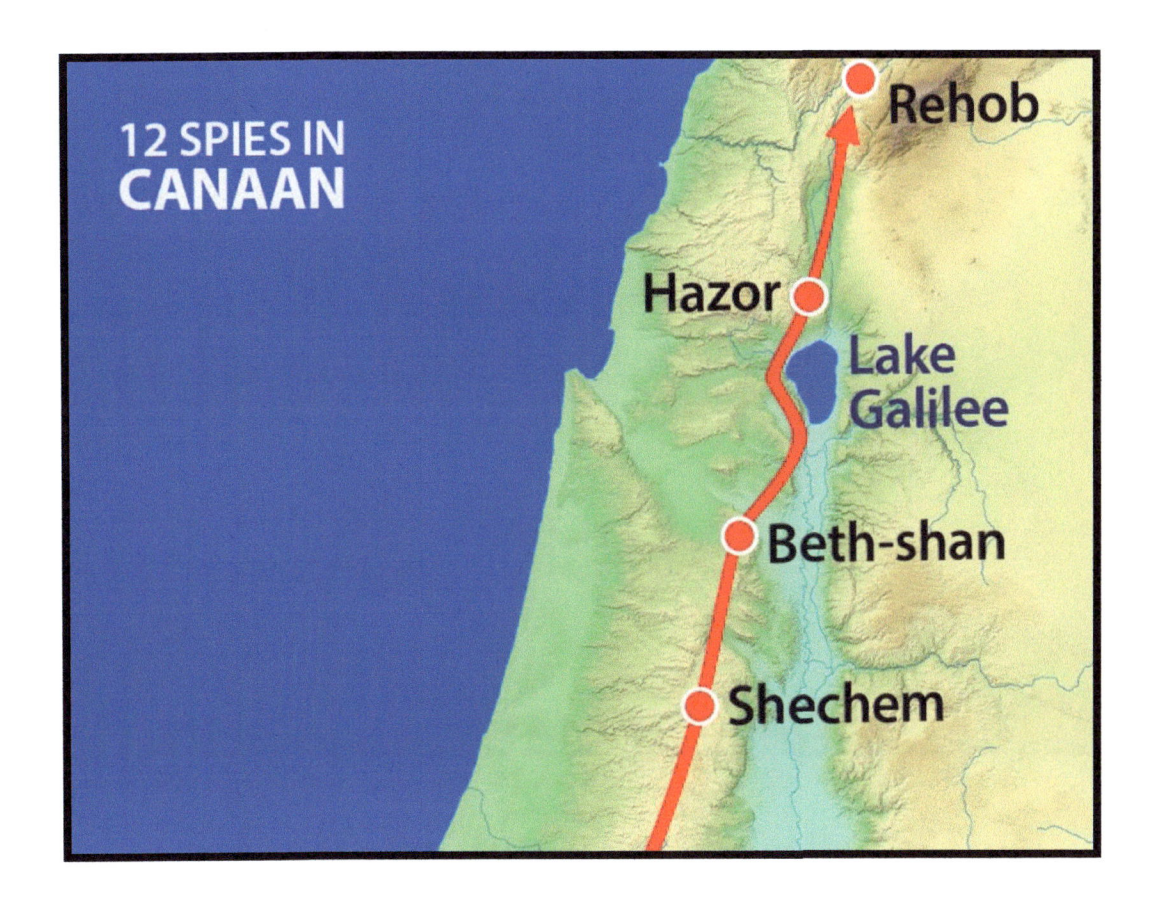

Numbers and Deuteronomy: A Comic Book of Doggerel

**They went as far as Rehob before returning.
All the time they were extremely discerning.**

In the Valley of Eshkol, they cut off grapes.
They tried hard to avoid any nasty scrapes.

They also carried pomegranates and tasty figs.
They might also have brought along some pigs.

Numbers and Deuteronomy: A Comic Book of Doggerel

After forty days, they returned home in good speed.
If cities are fortified, Caleb said, we can still succeed.

**Ten of the spies strongly disagreed.
All the people are huge like steeds.**

Numbers and Deuteronomy: A Comic Book of Doggerel

"What else is new?" the people once again grumbled.
They wanted another leader and were not humbled.

Joshua and Caleb said, "The land is really good!
There is plenty of honey and outstanding food."

"Let's not rebel against God or be afraid.
We recommend Hebrews go on a raid."

As some said, "Stone Caleb and Joshua!" God appeared.
Whiny Israelites thought he had already disappeared.

Fred Wurlitzer

**At the Tent of Meeting , God affirmed.
"Your love of me you often adjourned."**

**"You have wandered in the Sinai for forty years.
You suffered hardships without giving me cheers."**

Numbers and Deuteronomy: A Comic Book of Doggerel

There was one year for each day the spies were gone.
"Don't you realize I will not be by Hebrews outdone?"

"I made Hebrews strong. There will be justice!
When you whined, my glory was still lustrous."

The ten spies who gave a bad report died of plague.
People had plagues when they felt God was vague.

Caleb and Joshua survived as they trusted the Lord.
But still not all trusted in the Lord to come aboard.

The rebellious people changed their minds.
They wanted to leave Moses far, far behind.

Moses said, "We will attack the Amalekites!
They are just north of our camp. We'll fight."

Many Hebrews wanted to run.
They felt they were outdone.

**The Amalekites helped by Canaanites attacked.
Pushed into a swift retreat, Israelites cracked.**

Numbers and Deuteronomy: A Comic Book of Doggerel

The next forty years, Hebrews in deserts wandered.
A new generation came led by Joshua conquered.

They were under the leadership of Joshua.
The Israelites luckily gave him their hoorah.

Caleb gave his whole support.
In effect, he was a fine escort.

Numbers and Deuteronomy: A Comic Book of Doggerel

The Serpent of Brass

Numbers 13:26-14:45, 20:1-21:8

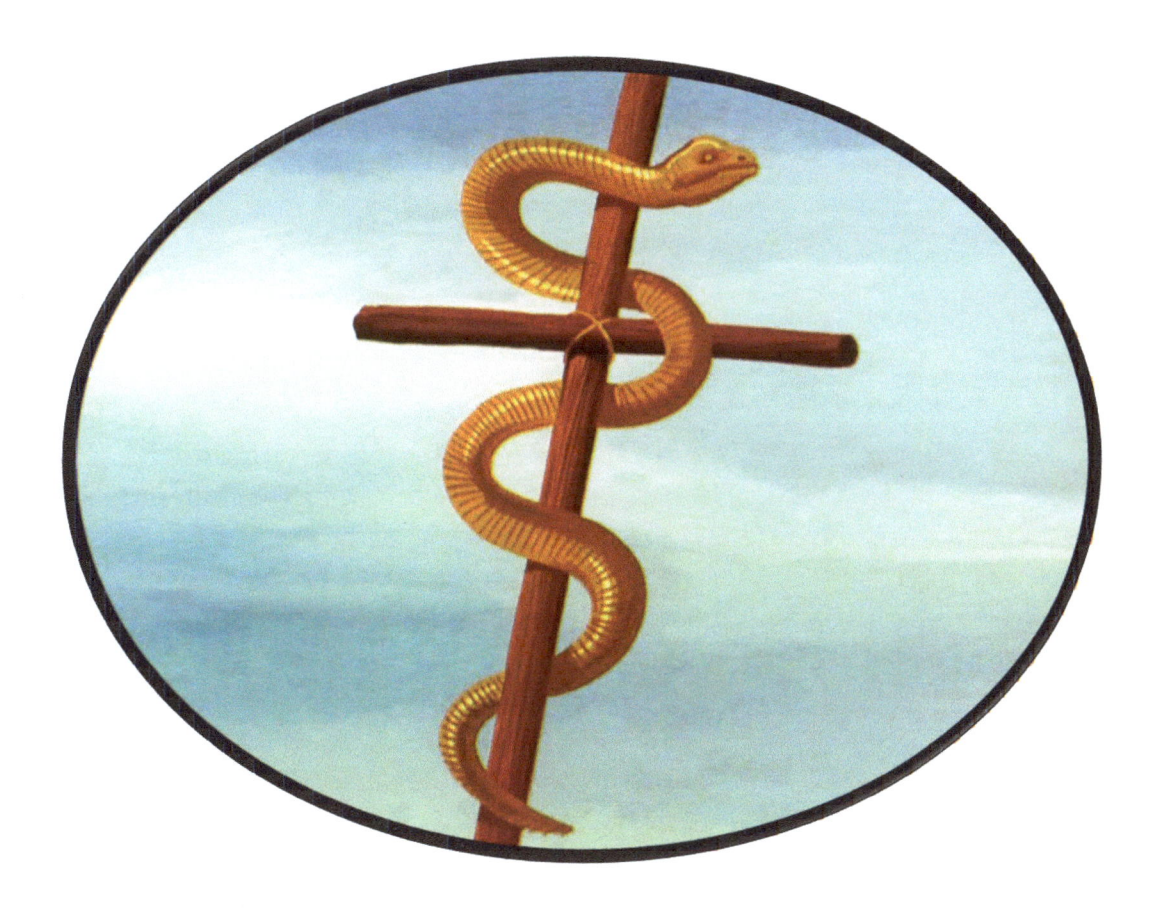

**Through Moses, God made the people free of Egypt.
In a new land, God said they would never be gypped.**

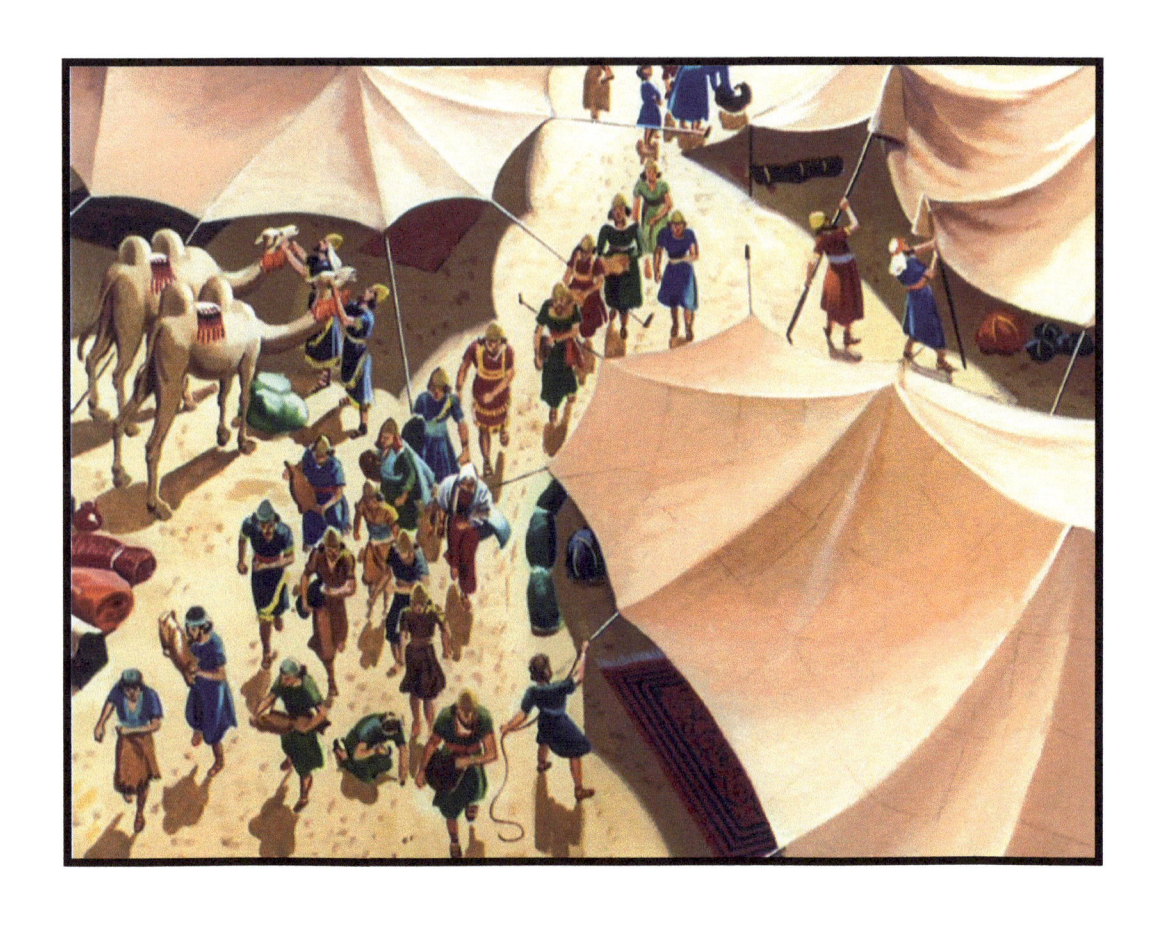

In Kadesh, in the Desert of Paran, they pitched tents.
Taking Canaan would be difficult, as told by portents.

Numbers and Deuteronomy: A Comic Book of Doggerel

The people suggested choosing a new-made leader.
He could guide them to Egypt as Moses' successor.

So, the Lord said, "These Israelites are truly unworthy. Only their children can see Canaan as trust worthies."

Turning their backs on God caused many troubles.
They could not find water and avoid health struggles.

They complained to Moses saying he was a disgrace.
"We'd rather be dead than stay in this dreadful place."

Numbers and Deuteronomy: A Comic Book of Doggerel

God told Moses to strike at Hebron a rock.
"It will pour out fresh water as if from a loch."

But multiple other problems occurred, too.
Edomite fierce warriors couldn't be wooed.

Numbers and Deuteronomy: A Comic Book of Doggerel

**Moses asked the King of Edom to allow his travel through.
The King said, "If you enter my land, your army I'll subdue!"**

So, Moses led the people from Edom to Mount Horeb. Then there was greater danger, in fact, a huge flareup.

Numbers and Deuteronomy: A Comic Book of Doggerel

**This time the Canaanite army swarmed towards them
It seemed the Hebrews would suffer shortly mayhem.**

Helpless against such an army, people turned to God.
God responded saying, "Canaanites will feel My rod."

A terrible battle ensued, and God gave Israel a victory.
Still the people grumbled with behavior contradictory.

Fred Wurlitzer

**They complained of fatigue and no water.
They even whined about manna and seder.**

The people further criticized Moses and their God.
God said, "Rebellion is a sin that gets not my nod."

Suddenly serpents swarmed in among the Israelites. There was no escape from the many dangerous bites.

Numbers and Deuteronomy: A Comic Book of Doggerel

**Numerous Israelites were dying.
They asked Moses to keep trying.**

They pleaded, "Take away these awful serpents.
We promise to be ever God's obedient servants."

Moses built at God's command a big brass serpent.
"All who look at it will be saved; that's my sermon."

Those who refused to look, died.
Those who looked then, survived.

Numbers and Deuteronomy: A Comic Book of Doggerel

DEUTERONOMY

Numbers and Deuteronomy: A Comic Book of Doggerel

Moses Dies and Joshua Becomes Leader

Deuteronomy 31-34 and Joshua 1:1-9

Numbers and Deuteronomy: A Comic Book of Doggerel

Moses addressed the Hebrew people.
This was not done from a high steeple.

"I am 120 years genuinely old.
We must our leadership remold."

"I will not cross the Jordan.
At times I feel like a warden."

Fred Wurlitzer

"I will not see the Promised Land.
I won't be able to unite our Band."

"You will conquer the Promised Land.
You will do this without me at hand."

Numbers and Deuteronomy: A Comic Book of Doggerel

Then Moses summoned Joshua.
"You will be a savior like Manna."

"Be strong, Be courageous.
Be always very audacious."

Fred Wurlitzer

"You will lead our people.
Be always like an eagle."

Numbers and Deuteronomy: A Comic Book of Doggerel

Moses then said further to Joshua:

"The Lord will not forsake you.
Let Him stick to you like glue."

Fred Wurlitzer

**Moses wrote again the laws.
He didn't miss any clauses.**

"Read them now every seven years."
"Put away fears with good cheers."

"This you will do at the Festival of Tabernacles."
There justice and wonders should truly sparkle.

**God then appeared at the Tabernacle entrance.
There people felt acceptance of His ascendance.**

Numbers and Deuteronomy: A Comic Book of Doggerel

But God predicted Hebrews would still disobey Him.
Unless they learned hymns of praise, it would be grim.

They would worship gods and be in the wrong.
God instructed Moses to write down His song.

**Moses recited it to the people to learn.
They should have no other concerns.**

**The words are in Deuteronomy Chapter Thirty-Two.
It was for Hebrew wisdom an immense breakthrough.**

The song told of God's greatness.
It sang of His boundless brightness

God would lead them to victory.
The rest would remain as history.

Fred Wurlitzer

God said to Moses, "Go to Mount Nebo."
There you will see my panoramic show."

"Look from there at the Promised Land of Canaan.
Don't for even a moment let your happiness rein in."

"After you see the land, you must then die.
Sometimes, you did not My lessons apply."

"That is because you oft resisted my instructions.
You sinned when you made your own deductions."

"At Meribahkadesh, you made no water.
You became your own personal plotter."

Fred Wurlitzer

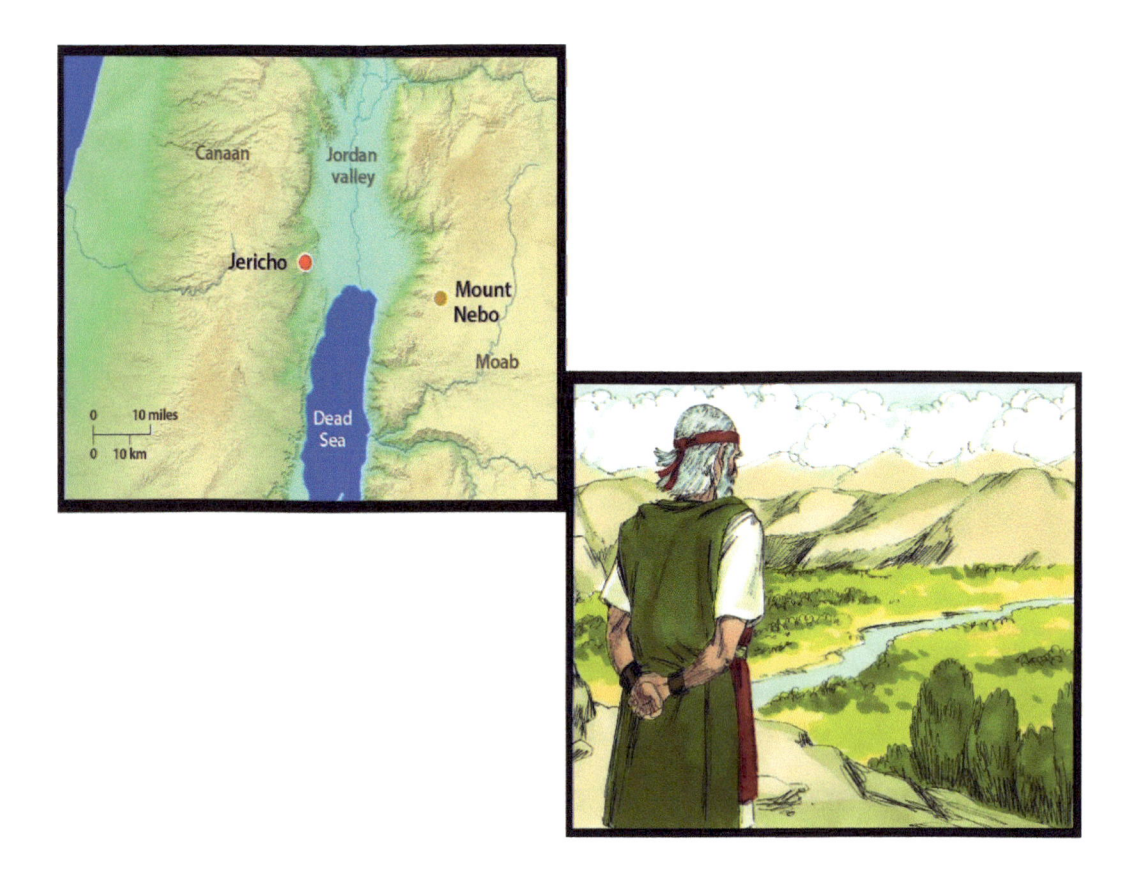

**From Pisgah Peak on Mount Nebo, Moses saw Canaan.
From the Jordan to Jericho, Hebrews would reign in.**

So Moses died in Moab for God a legal perfectionist.
When he died, he was strong and eyesight excellent.

He had gathered laws later collated in Leviticus.
A legal foundation was constructed without fuss.

The Israelites learned what to do to behave.
They had freedom to also become depraved.

Fred Wurlitzer

If they followed God, they would probably be saved.
But if they took other gods they could be enslaved.

For forty years Moses listened to Hebrews whining.
Yet, his endurance never appeared to be declining.

Often his patience was sadly tested.
But with God, he was never bested.

Numbers and Deuteronomy: A Comic Book of Doggerel

**The people mourned Moses for thirty days.
Only God could have given him more praise.**

**No other has ever talked to God face to face.
He was, through great God, given much grace.**

Fred Wurlitzer

Joshua was full of wisdom.
He still suffered criticism.

Numbers and Deuteronomy: A Comic Book of Doggerel

God said, "Lead my people across the broad Jordan.
I will neither abandon you nor Hebrew land board in."

"Remember the laws day and night.
Banish fears and doubts with might."

Fred Wurlitzer

"I will be with you wherever you might go.
Together, you and I will put on a good show."